The Usborne
Very First
Dictionary

Felicity Brooks and Caroline Young

Illustrated by Jo Litchfield

Contents

Here are some children you will meet in this book.

Ellie   Ben   Molly   Polly Jack   Robert   Laura   Olly Emily

Designed by Francesca Allen and Keith Newell

SCHOLASTIC INC.

New York Toronto London Auckland Sydney
Mexico City New Delhi Hong Kong Buenos Aires

Aa

afternoon

The sun is out this **afternoon**.

all

They are **all** playing music.

about

The boy reads **about** school.

again

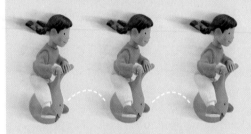

The little girl bounces
again and **again**.

alphabet

abcdefgh
ijklmnopq
rstuvwxyz

Do you know the **alphabet**?

after

One twin
goes **after**
the other.

air

Balloons float in the **air**.

always

Tom **always** wears socks.

ambulance

This **ambulance** is taking a boy to the hospital.

animal

These **animals** live on the farm.

ant

Ants have six legs.

angel

This **angel** has white wings.

ankle

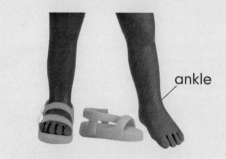

ankle

Ankles are above feet.

any

Is there **any** soup in the pot?

angry

This girl looks **angry**.

another

This boy wants **another** drink.

apple

Here's a shiny red **apple**.

are

These monkeys **are** hungry.

asleep

Shhh, the little boy's **asleep.**

Bb

arm

arm

Ben is looking at his **arm.**

astronaut

Astronauts go into space.

baby

This **baby** is happy.

ask

The girl **asks** who's on the phone.

awake

The children are still **awake.**

bad

This apple is **bad.**

bag

This **bag** has flowers on it.

banana

Ripe **bananas** are yellow.

beach

The children love the **beach**.

ball

This **ball** is made of plastic.

basket

There's bread in this **basket**.

bear

Here's a big brown **bear**.

balloon

Each child has a **balloon**.

bath

Do you enjoy a **bath**?

bed

Who is in the **bed**?

bee

Some **bees** make honey.

big

Swans are **big** birds.

bite

The boy is taking a big **bite**.

belt

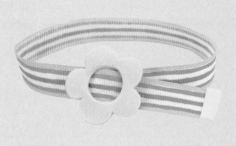

Here's a pretty **belt**.

bird

This **bird** is blue and white.

blanket

Blankets keep you warm in bed.

bicycle

Can you ride a **bicycle**?

birthday

This is a **birthday** cake.

boat

Dad likes his little **boat**.

bone

You can see this boy's **bones** on the x-ray.

bowl

There is salad in this **bowl**.

bread

This is a loaf of **bread**.

book

Farm

This **book** is about farms.

box

What is in the **box**?

breakfast

What's for **breakfast**?

boot

Do you like these **boots**?

boy

This **boy** is playing.

brother

These **boys** are **brothers**.

brush

Do you use a
brush for your hair?

butterfly

Butterflies are very pretty.

Cc

build

The men **build** a wall.

button

These **buttons** are plastic.

cake

This **cake** looks delicious.

bus

The **bus** comes at
one o'clock.

buy

The boy is **buying** candy.

can

How many girls
can you see?

car

This is a shiny blue car.

cat

This is an orange cat.

cheese

Do you like cheese?

b
c

carrot

Carrots are vegetables.

catch

"Catch!" says the boy.

cherry

Cherries are small fruit.

castle

This is a fairytale castle.

chair

Here's a red chair.

chicken

Chickens live on farms.

chocolate

Do you like chocolate?

cloud

There's a cloud in the sky.

come

The clown comes through the door.

clock

A clock shows the time.

coat

The vet has a white coat.

computer

This is a new computer.

clothes

The children are wearing warm clothes.

cold

It's cold in winter.

cook

A chef's job is to cook.

cow

Milk comes from cows.

Dd

day

The sun rises every day.

cry

The little boy is crying because his ear hurts.

dance

This girl loves to dance.

deep

Diggers make deep holes.

cup

This cup has a picture on it.

dark

It's dark at night.

dentist

Dentists look at your teeth.

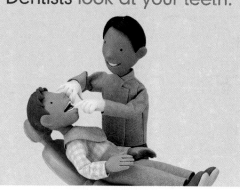

dig

Anna is **digging**.

dirty

This **digger** is **dirty**.

dog

This **dog** is friendly.

digger

This is a clean **digger**.

do

There's lots to **do** at the beach.

doll

This **doll** has yellow hair.

dinosaur

Do you like **dinosaurs**?

doctor

The **doctor** is looking in the little boy's ear.

donkey

Donkeys have big ears.

door

This **door** is pink.

dress

This is a party **dress**.

drum

The boy is playing a **drum**.

dragon

Dragons have wings.

drink

This woman needs a **drink**.

dry

A towel helps you get **dry**.

draw

This girl likes **drawing**.

drive

This woman **drives** to work.

duck

Ducks can swim.

Ee

ear

Polly points to Jack's **ear**.

egg

There are three blue **eggs** in this nest.

each

Each child has a toy car.

Earth

The **Earth** looks like this from space.

elbow

—elbow

This is Ben's **elbow**.

eagle

Eagles are large birds.

eat

This boy likes **eating** pasta.

elephant

Elephants are very big.

empty

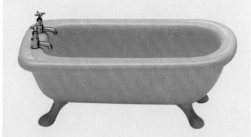

The bathtub is **empty**.

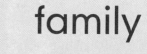

family

How big is this **family**?

end

There's one girl at each **end**.

face

Here's a happy **face**.

farm

This family lives on a **farm**.

eye

Jack points to Polly's **eye**.

fairy

Fairies can fly.

fast

This car goes very **fast**.

fat

This cat is **fat**.

fire engine

Many **fire engines** are red.

flag

This is the French **flag**.

finger

finger

Which **finger** is Ellie holding up?

firefighter

Firefighters wear uniforms.

floor

There's a toy on the **floor**.

fire

This is a log **fire**.

fish

Fish live in water.

flower

This **flower** has blue petals.

fly

These birds are **flying**.

forest

Trees grow in a **forest**.

friend

This girl's dog is her **friend**.

food

Look at all this **food**!

fork

Can you use a **fork**?

frog

This **frog** is on a leaf.

foot

foot

You kick with your **feet**.

fox

Foxes come out at night.

fruit

This is a bowl of **fruit**.

f

G g

gate
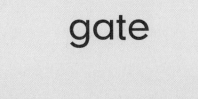
The **gate** is closed.

giraffe

Giraffes are very tall.

game

What **game** do they play?

ghost

This **ghost** is white.

girl

These **girls** are all friends.

garden

Do you have a **garden**?

giant

Giants are big people.

give

Molly **gives** her friend a present.

G

glass

How many **glasses** can you see here?

go

This bus **goes** to the supermarket.

goldfish

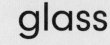

Goldfish make good pets.

glasses

This man wears **glasses**.

goat

Here are two **goats**.

good

These cupcakes look **good**.

gloves

This is a pair of **gloves**.

gold

Look at all this **gold**!

goose

Geese have big feet.

grapes

Here are some **grapes**.

grow

Flowers **grow** in the ground.

Hh

grass

The balls are on the **grass**.

grown-up

Dads are **grown-ups**.

hair

hair——

Ellie has pretty **hair**.

ground

The girl falls on the **ground**.

guinea pig

Guinea pigs are good pets.

hamster

This **hamster** has a bad eye.

hand

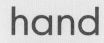

hand

Polly is waving her **hand**.

hat

She has a pretty **hat**.

helicopter

This **helicopter** helps rescue people.

happy

Polly and Jack are **happy**.

head

Here is Ben's **head**.

help

The nurse is **helping** the little boy.

hard

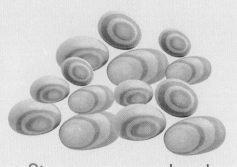

Stones are very **hard**.

hear

Jack can **hear** something.

hide

The clown is **hiding** behind the chair.

hit

This girl is **hitting** the ball.

honey

Honey comes from bees.

horse

This **horse** has a foal.

hole

This cheese has **holes** in it.

hood

This coat has a **hood**.

hospital

This **hospital** is small.

home

Everyone is at **home** today.

hop

Can you **hop**?

hot

Careful! The pans are **hot**.

house

This **house** has a red door.

Ii

idea

This boy has an **idea**.

hug

The little boy **hugs** his bear.

ice

Ice is very cold.

if

If it rains, you need an umbrella.

hurt

The boy's arm **hurts**.

ice cream

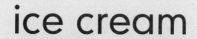

Ice cream is delicious.

ink

This pen has green **ink**.

insect

Insects have six legs.

is

This woman is hungry.

Jj

invitation

Olivia invites
Francesca
to her birthday party on
February 15 at 3 o'clock.
RSVP

This is an invitation to a birthday party.

island

This is a small island.

jacket

This is a blue jacket.

iron

This iron is very hot.

itch

This dog has an itch.

jar

These are jars of jelly.

jeans

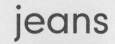

Jeans are often blue.

jigsaw puzzle

These girls are doing a jigsaw puzzle.

juice

This is orange juice.

jewel

There are red jewels on the king's crown.

job

Vicky has a job as a vet.

jump

One cat jumps off the sofa.

jewelry

This jewelry is in a box.

juggle

The clown can juggle.

jungle

There are trees in a jungle.

i
j

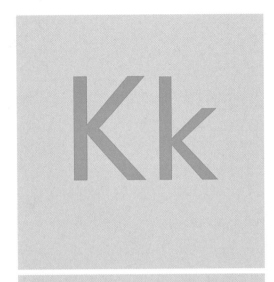

Kk

key

This is the **key** to someone's house.

kiss

His mum gives him a **kiss**.

kangaroo

Kangaroos have long tails.

kick

The boys **kick** the ball.

kitchen

The chefs are in the **kitchen**.

ketchup

This is a bottle of **ketchup**.

king

This **king** has long hair.

kite

Kites fly in the sky.

kitten

What cute little **kittens!**

Ll

lamp

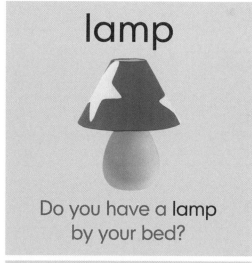

Do you have a **lamp** by your bed?

knee

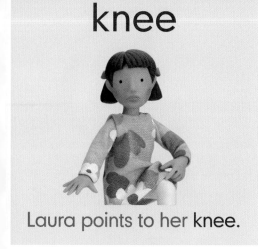

Laura points to her **knee.**

ladybug

Ladybugs are insects.

laugh

The children are **laughing.**

knife

You use a **knife** to cut food.

lamb

Lambs like to run and jump.

leaf

Most **leaves** are green.

k
l

leg

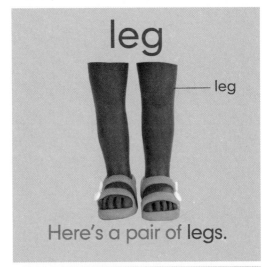

leg

Here's a pair of **legs**.

letter

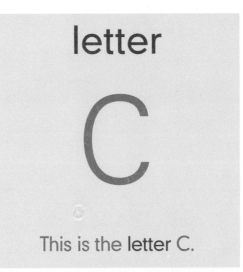

C

This is the **letter** C.

like

Cats **like** playing.

lemon

Lemons are yellow fruit.

lie

This girl has to **lie** in bed.

lion

Lions live in Africa.

let

The girl **lets** her friend ride her scooter.

light

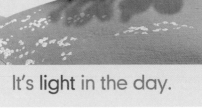

It's **light** in the day.

lips

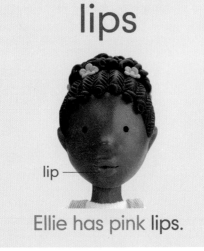
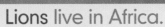

lip

Ellie has pink **lips**.

L

listen

Jack is **listening** to a noise.

long

This girl has **long** hair.

loud

WOOF WOOF!

The dog's bark is very **loud**.

little

He's **little**; she's quite big.

look

The children are **looking** at the picture.

love

The children **love** painting.

live

A family **lives** here.

lots

Spotty has **lots** of puppies.

lunch

These people eat **lunch** at 12 o'clock.

Mm

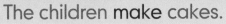
make

The children **make** cakes.

mermaid

Mermaids have fish tails.

machine

This **machine** washes clothes.

man

This **man** has a dog.

mess

What a **mess**!

magic

Witches can do **magic**.

map

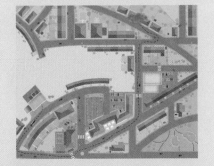

This is a **map** of a town.

milk

Most **milk** comes from cows.

M

mirror

Jack's looking in the **mirror**.

monster

This **monster** looks sad.

morning

The sun rises in the **morning**.

money

Coins and bills are **money**.

moon

You see the **moon** at night.

motorcycle

Motorcycles can go fast.

monkey

This is a funny **monkey**!

more

Which arm has **more** birds on it?

mountain

There's snow on the top of this **mountain**.

m

mouse

This **mouse** has pink ears.

mud

The girl has **mud** on her.

Nn

mouth

mouth

You open your **mouth** to eat.

mushroom

Do you like **mushrooms**?

name

This girl's **name** is Olivia.

move

The boys are trying to **move** the big package.

music

This man is playing **music**.

naughty

This dog is **naughty**.

near

The tractor is **near** the wall.

need

This boy **needs** boots today.

nest

There are birds in this **nest**.

neck

neck

This is Ben's **neck**.

needle

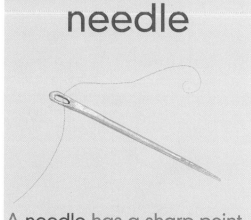

A **needle** has a sharp point.

net

There's a crab in this girl's **net**.

necklace

What a pretty **necklace**!

neighbor

Neighbors live next to each other.

never

Never play with matches.

m
n

new

This is a **new** red bag.

nobody

Nobody lives on this planet.

not

This boy is **not** feeling well.

newspaper

This is an old **newspaper**.

noise

Babies make lots of **noise**.

nothing

There's **nothing** in his box.

night

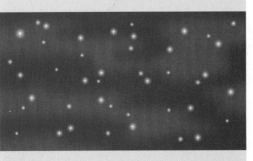

You can see stars at **night**.

nose

nose

This man has a red **nose**.

now

There are four children here **now**.

number

This is the **number** 5.

Oo

of

Would you like a glass **of** juice?

nurse

The **nurse** helps the girl.

o'clock

This clock says 3 **o'clock**.

often

The girl **often** takes the dog for a walk.

nut

Nuts have hard shells.

octopus

An **octopus** has eight arms.

oil

This is a bottle of **oil**.

old

These people are **old**.

only

The orange cat has **only** one cushion.

orange

Oranges are juicy.

once

This boy takes a shower **once** a day.

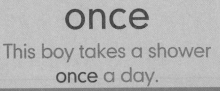

open

Alice is **opening** the door.

other

Where is his **other** sock?

onion

Do you like eating **onions**?

or

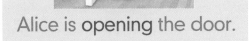

Do you want pasta **or** soup?

owl

Owls come out at night.

Pp

palace

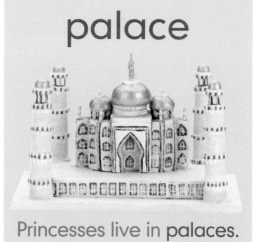

Princesses live in **palaces**.

park

Children play in the **park**.

page

The girl likes this **page** best.

panda

Pandas live in forests.

party

It's Polly's birthday **party**.

paint

This artist is **painting** trees.

paper

This boy is folding **paper**.

pasta

You can buy **pasta** in bags.

o
p

peach

Peaches have soft skins.

pen

How many pens are here?

people

There are lots of people at the market.

pear

Pears are good to eat.

pencil

You can draw with a pencil.

pet

Do you have a pet?

peas

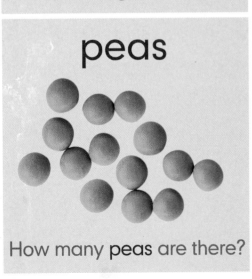

How many peas are there?

penguin

Penguins can't fly.

piano

This man plays the piano.

P

picnic

They are having a **picnic**.

pillow

Do you have a soft **pillow**?

plane

This is a toy **plane**.

picture

What's in this **picture**?

pirate

These children are dressed as **pirates**.

plant

This **plant** has a small pot.

piece

Would you like a **piece** of cake?

pizza

This **pizza** looks good.

plate

There's food on this **plate**.

p

play

The children **play** together.

pocket

This boy is putting his hands in his **pockets**.

present

Who are these **presents** for?

playground

The **playground** is full of people.

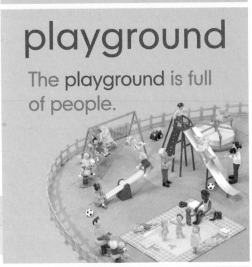

police officer

POLICE

Here are two **police officers**.

pretty

These flowers look **pretty**.

plum

Ripe **plums** are juicy.

potato

Potatoes grow under the ground.

princess

This **princess** has curly hair.

prize

The **prize** is a silver cup.

puppy

This **puppy** has a red collar.

Qq

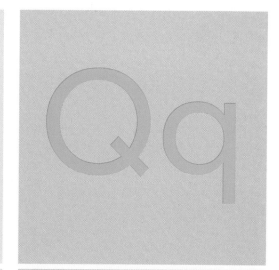

pull

The boy **pulls** the donkey.

push

This girl is **pushing** her doll.

queen

This **queen** has a red dress.

puppet

This girl has a **puppet**.

put

The doctor **puts** the baby down gently.

quiet

Quiet! The baby is sleeping.

p
q

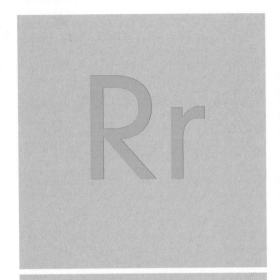

Rr

rain

You can't play in the **rain**.

rat

This **rat** has a pink tail.

rabbit

This **rabbit** has four babies.

rainbow

Can you paint a **rainbow**?

read

This girl enjoys **reading**.

radio

Do you like listening to the **radio**?

raspberry

Raspberries are soft fruit.

remember

A list helps you **remember** what to buy.

rice

Do you like **rice**?

river

river

A big **river** runs through the town.

rocket

This is a toy **rocket**.

ride

Emily is **riding** a pony.

road

They are crossing the **road**.

roof

This house has a red **roof**.

ring

Which **ring** do you like best?

robot

Look at this **robot**!

room

This **room** is a mess!

rope

This is strong **rope**.

Ss

sandwich

This **sandwich** looks good.

round

Balls are usually **round**.

sad

This little boy looks **sad**.

say

The woman **says** she can't find her dog.

run

The dogs **run** in the street.

sand

There's **sand** in this desert.

scarf

This is a nice warm **scarf**.

R
S

school

This is a small **school**.

secret

This girl is telling her friend a **secret**.

share

They are **sharing** some fruit.

scissors

You use **scissors** for cutting.

see

The firefighter **sees** a dog.

sheep

Sheep like eating grass.

sea

Lots of plants and animals live in the **sea**.

sell

This woman **sells** fruit.

ship

Cars can go on this **ship**.

r

s

shoe

These are new **shoes**.

show

Polly **shows** her dad her toy.

sister

These girls are **sisters**.

short

This girl has **short** hair.

silver

This fish is **silver**.

sit

They are **sitting** on stools.

shout

Fido! Fido!

The boys are **shouting**.

sing

This woman loves **singing**.

skin

This boy's **skin** is pink.

S

skirt

This **skirt** is blue.

slow

Tortoises are very **slow**.

smile

People usually **smile** for photographs.

sky

Planes fly in the **sky**.

small

The green fish is **small**.

snail

Snails move very slowly.

sleep

This boy wants to **sleep**.

smell

The cat can **smell** the fish.

snake

Some snakes live in trees.

snow

There is **snow** on this tree.

sofa

There are cats on this **sofa**.

spider

A **spider** has eight legs.

so

This woman is **so** surprised.

soft

This blanket is very **soft**.

spoon

This is a baby's **spoon**.

soap

This is a bar of **soap**.

some

The cat needs **some** help.

stand

These people are **standing** at the bus stop.

S

star

You see **stars** at night.

story

What is this **story** about?

sun

The **sun** is very hot.

start

The party **starts** at 3 o'clock.

strawberry

Do you like **strawberries**?

supermarket

Supermarkets sell food.

stop

Cars have to **stop** here.

street

This **street** is full of people.

swim

This boy loves **swimming**.

T t

take

The man **takes** the box.

teacher

Miss Sims is a **teacher**.

table

This **table** is green.

talk

These women are **talking** about food.

teddy bear

This **teddy bear** is brown.

tail

Dogs often wag their **tails**.

tall

Emily is **tall** for her age.

teeth

This girl has white **teeth**.

teeth

T

telephone

The doctor is talking
on the **telephone**.

throw

This boy likes
throwing snowballs.

time

What **time** is it?

television

Do you like
watching **television**?

thumb

— thumb

Ben holds up his left **thumb**.

tired

The boy's too **tired** to walk.

thing

What is that **thing**?

tiger

Tigers live in jungles.

toe

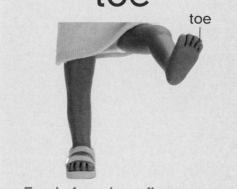

toe

Each foot has five **toes**.

t

tomato

This **tomato** is ripe.

town

This is a small **town**.

train

This is an old **train**.

tongue

This boy's **tongue** is pink.

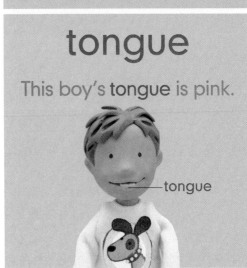

—tongue

toy

This dog is a **toy**.

tree

Trees grow in the ground.

towel

This girl has a pink **towel**.

tractor

Tractors work on farms.

truck

This is a big red **truck**.

T
U
V

Uu

ugly

This fish is very **ugly**.

umbrella

This boy uses an **umbrella** when it rains.

Vv

vase

Here is a **vase** of flowers.

vegetable

Do you know the names of all these **vegetables**?

very

Firefighters are **very** brave.

visit

A clown is coming to **visit**.

voice

This boy has a good **voice**.

t
u
v

Ww

walk

Do you **walk** to school?

warm

These children have **warm** clothes on.

wait

These people are all **waiting** to see a doctor.

wall

The builders make a **wall**.

wash

You can **wash** in the bathtub.

wake up

ring! ring!

It's time to **wake up**!

want

The puppy **wants** to play.

watch

This is a yellow **watch**.

water

This is a bottle of water.

wet

This man is all wet!

whisper

The boy is whispering.

wave

These people are waving.

whale

Whales live in the sea.

win

Who do you think is winning?

wear

Chefs wear tall hats.

wheel

This is the wheel of a car.

window

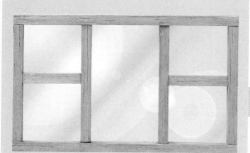

This window is closed.

W

wing

This insect has big **wings**.

work

They **work** in a restaurant.

Xx

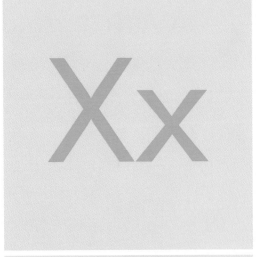

with

This girl is **with** her mom.

worm

Worms are often pink.

x-ray

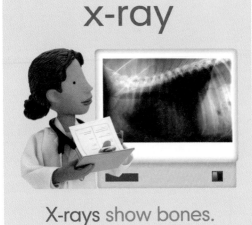

X-rays show bones.

woman

This **woman** is named Sally.

write

This girl is **writing** her name.

xylophone

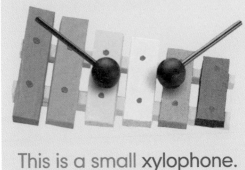

This is a small **xylophone**.

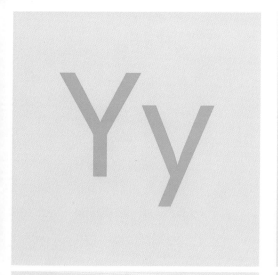
Yy

yet
This baby can't walk **yet**.

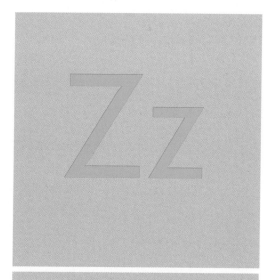
Zz

yawn

You **yawn** when you're tired.

yogurt

This is raspberry **yogurt**.

zebra

Zebras are black and white.

year

This baby is less than a **year** old.

young

A foal is a **young** horse.

zipper
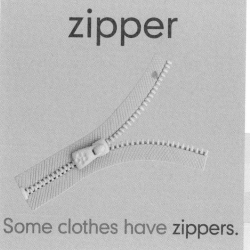
Some clothes have **zippers**.

W
X
Y
Z

Where are they?

These two pages show some words you use when you want to say where someone or something is.

behind

The boy is **behind** the girl.

in

What's **in** the top drawer?

above

The plane is flying **above** the clouds.

between

The little boy is **between** two grown-ups.

in front of

The cars are **in front of** the house.

across

Don't run **across** the road!

here/there

I'm **here**; he's over **there**.

inside

There are people **inside** the house.

into

Emily is putting the duckling **into** the pond.

opposite

The man is sitting **opposite** the woman.

to/from

Anna goes **from** her house **to** school.

next to

Patch is sitting **next to** Ted.

outside

Animal Hospital

These people are **outside** the hospital.

under

Molly is **under** the table.

on

The little girl is lying **on** the doctor's table.

over

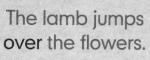

The lamb jumps **over** the flowers.

up/down

One girl is **up** when the other is **down**.

Me, you and them

This page shows some words you use when you want to talk about yourself, other people, or things.

he/him/his

He has his sister with him.

we/us/our

We have our bags with us.

I/me/my

I have my brother with me.

she/her

She has her doll with her.

you/your

Do you have all your lambs with you?

you/your

Do you have your hat with you?

it/its

It always has its shell with it.

they/them/their

They have all their dogs with them.

Question words

This page shows some of the words you can use when you want to ask a question about something.

what

What is she reading?

which

Which dog do you like best?

how

How do you make a cake?

when

When does the bus come?

who

Who is that singing?

how many

How many shells can you see?

where

Where are his friends?

why

Why is Laura sad?

Colors

white

blue

yellow

purple

pink

green

orange

red

gray

black

brown

Shapes

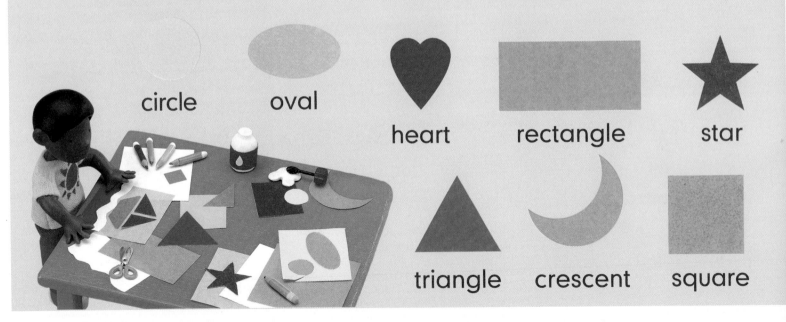

circle

oval

heart

rectangle

star

triangle

crescent

square

Numbers

1 one

2 two

3 three

4 four

5 five

6 six

7 seven

8 eight

9 nine

10 ten

Months

January
February
March
April
May
June
July
August
September
October
November
December

Days

Monday
Tuesday
Wednesday
Thursday
Friday
Saturday
Sunday

yesterday
today
tomorrow

Seasons

Spring
Summer
Fall
Winter

Photography by Howard Allman & MMStudios

With thanks to Paul Allen, Ben Denne and Claire Masset, and to Staedtler UK for providing the Fimo® material for models. Vehicles supplied by Bruder® Toys.

ISBN 0-439-81507-X

12 11 10 9 8 7 6 5 4 3 2 1   5 6 7 8 9 10/0

Printed in the U.S.A.   40

First Scholastic printing, November 2005